Red Car

Patrick Playter Hartigan

Double Movement Publications

ISBN: 978-0-6152-4467-9

Design, production, and illustration by Patrick Playter Hartigan

Acknowledgments: Parts of this work were first read aloud at the Deadwood, in Iowa City, Iowa; other parts appeared in *The Pacific Coast Review*

Cover Illustration: *Poem Engine*, May, 2003, graphite stick on paper, by Patrick Playter Hartigan

Double Movement Publications
Patrick Playter Hartigan
2239 SE 47th Avenue
Portland, Oregon, 97215

Contents

1

2

For Endi

1

3 Days

dreamt blue
ocean green
skies black
lacing thru

chalk white
to highlite
so faceless
highlite to

ocean black
skied black
lacing thru
dreamt blue

reveille

tomorrow
is
tomorrow

tomorrow
thinks
tomorrow
thinks

I think
tomorrow
thinks
tomorrow
thinks
tomorrow
thinks.

I think
I think
I think
I think
tomorrow
thinks I
think
I think

```
tomorrow thinks
tomorrow is


tomorrow is
tomorrow thinks

tomorrow thinks
```

Cats and dogs invent things.
There was the crossed-agent,
fawning invective, practical
zoomers, a workshop dangling
from the setting sun: surfer
culture, periodontology. Men
unaccustomed to a discussion
of these issues may find the
going rough. Electric trains
& electric brains, also. Why
should history trade its mad
adumbrations for hapfulness?
Clippers, slippers, beatling
trippers. Negligence is that
domain posterior to unction.
Divested of each other's hap
at a PreCambrian flood; told
different things, accoutered
differently, no eye's not so
snug as it wouldn't be lured
by beauty. Raising to a tree
topped by fern-like growth a
shallow hand, flecked by ash
and what naturally falls, an
awkward and hardly unlikable
species founded on (say it):
reasoning (let us) interest.

RUST

A fictional account, in 12 unequal sections

what am I
a laborer
a laborer

they say I'm
universal
universal
I don't know

I don't know
a laborer
a laborer

a laborer
a laborer
a laborer

white
green
white
green

green
green
white
green

white
white
blues
white

green.
green
green
green

green.

white

blues
white.

green.
blues.

green
blues
white
green.

green.

I love you more than
love to be the dust of pigs and dust
is not my love.

How you live with me.

like this coming down,
fire money money fire.

Good throat.

Wildflowers opened.
That was my day.
I hope you
made enough.

I am
love
blue
blue
blue
blue

Look
the city's tallest building is a flag as yet
a flag.

I cannot tire.
Dust and it's a color.
Rust we call it and we call it rust.

On this,
what would have become the anniversary of
our having
left town together,
as we are not speaking,

And we are not speaking,
as time has lost its furry head,
oh do not think what of it.
I need sex and some above it.

mammallian adumbration:
block of the lines to line and city
flow.

No generality toward the greatest,
air.
I read your life,
my ankles crossed upon a quilt stitched with
care.

Air,
you have range.

She married and continued to produce.

Expect to be honest with how you are.

Where I work are people
who have lives of their own.

I have been a wonderful man.

Let's pretend a man starting again.

The margin of a margin that's a border
that's a blue.

"Hisself and the life of ponds,"
hand-stitched pants billowing,
glazing off the distance,
wrinkling, unresistant.

How does the soldier feel today?

(The soldier is chewing on air.)

```
time trouble
time & trouble

time & time
& time & trouble

trouble & time
trouble & time

time & time
& trouble & time


trouble
trouble
trouble


time.


trouble
trouble
time.


time.


time & trouble & time

trouble & time & time.

time & trouble.
time & trouble.
time &.
```

white times white is blue
is white x blue and
marries blue

white marries blue to
equal blue
& green is blue x blue x blue

green & blue is blue.

green and white is
blue and white:
green and white is blue.

green is white and blue.

white and blue has
marriages has
blue with white x green x white
divided by the sunsets
nights and blues for white has time.

white & blue has time for blue and white

blue & green is green and blue and white

blue and white is white & blue and white

organization consists of little ends in space

most of what I say has its beginning in space

space is a lesser word so we will employ less

blue for blue and white to blue and white to
blue and white

green from green is blue to green for green
for white to blue

blue for blue
blue for blue.

white from green toward white and green,
air,
air.

green the air and white the blue the blue
the.

green the air and blue the blue.

white with green.
white with green.

the air the blue the green the white the
air.

the air the air.
the air.

green for blue for blue for blue.

the white the blue.

the air the green the white the blue the air
the green.

listen if the city to the side.

shade of whether pond nor rain.

varied the tones skeletal tent.

she has a job now she has a job

plastic raptors dangle. ventage

tous les choses qui sont fameux

play to me in the manner of age

hemlock where, chestnut, gather

there or like wave before waves

2

Mythene

variety conscious
concision various

ever remarry just
register carry us

where I nefarious
blunder embarrass

staring hilarious
Hildegaard daring

Erosless carrying
instant repairing

Survival Guide

Let's not, for some time, read who we like.
A town, the streets of which are lined with
marigolds. We can work apart for four days,

The moon will tire, looking like a cuticle.
Gas tank, hour, needles; otherwise needles.
I'll buy a pick-up truck. A big & blue one.

I think we have a problem. It is beautiful.
Killing a porcupine may take some climbing.
Moss around a tree; bears that cannot read.

I thought to think a little thought today--
and so it clicked, startled out from habit,
how lovers, hunters, wish at hits tomorrow.

Second book, first poem

A man who smokes dreaming of oranges
rarely should be held to account for
extremities of verbal management nor
will he relax in the naming of ships

No, no. He it will be who we mark as
defender of landslides & fruitiness;
a counter; a top-side sea inspector;
calvalcade dean; opus thrumbulatore.

Words are not pigeons, Words can not
hit the spots. Your inquiries arrest
the spirit of a century whose unrest
ambuciliates with flaring nakedness.

Yes, yes. I am awarding the physical
signature sweep. Otherwise the paper
darts mountainways: a million colors
vocalize waking Terpsichore's train.

Speak, Mr. Zoom-Zoom

The city is not a sandwich.

Trees don't point anything.

Girls are never like girls.

Earth's capital is Honesty.

Yellow roses savor leafery.

Bookstores are our enemies.

Folks don't visit, no more.

Dangerous, these centuries.

Amplitude Including

A discussion of politics is not complete
without. Blue Heron, in your vacillitude
do you think of me? All the dim weather.
Radios detach easily with thumb pressure
. Am I in position to accelerate, master
? We will reclaim the village green: our
modest determination will be our legacy.
blue green yellow green blue green brown
She had acquired the habit of massaging.
Her delicate wrist with her right thumb.
How can you begin to fish in such weathe
r? I was fond, as a child, of geometry.
Any quality literally just fascinates me.

Allegio

        deserts and mountains &
        deserts and mountains &
        deserts and mountains & streams.

        deserts and streams,
        deserts and streams.

        mountains and deserts &
        mountains and deserts &
        deserts and mountains & streams.

        mountains and deserts and streams.
        mountains and deserts and streams.

        mountains and mountains &
        mountains and mountains &
        mountains and deserts and streams.

        mountains and mountains &
        deserts and mountains &
        deserts and mountains and streams.

        deserts and streams,
        deserts and deserts and deserts and streams.

        deserts and streams,
        deserts and deserts and streams
        and streams,
        deserts and mountains and streams,
        and streams.

deserts and mountains,
streams and mountains,
deserts and deserts &
mountains & deserts &
deserts and mountains and streams,
and streams, &
deserts and deserts and mountains and
deserts and streams.

In Concert

We would like to magnify
the telephone. Stand up,
please. We would like to
amplify the unicorn. Get
to your feet. Cancel the
remainder of these daily
interchanges with purple
ambition. Bare-footedly,
flee from yawping horde;
scrub Titanic for ardor.
Indifference is the cell
-ophane choking bullets.
You like the bullet. Lip
after your partner--I am
distance and those stars
--. Days through a woods
evolve into night-words:
you bridge mountains You
talk me down from bridge
-guaranteed figurations.
Indifference is the cell
-uloid capstan of bliss.
The folowing succession
of women should interest
men of every description
Time allowing of course.
They said it was perfect
and nothing has been so.
Recollection chases cell
-ularity. Reasoning is a
hunter who operates solo
on the heels of a storm.

Red Car

America: likes
cooking smarts
& steamy parts
& legal starts

I like America
I like you Ame
rica likes you
I like America

America can be
instances with
nice and clean
& red as rain.

Once upon time
legend snoring
bellyful child
takestowhoring

happily crumbs
wasted; thumbs
tasting of pie
ain't so dumb.

How do I live?
A nice red car
jumps the curb
smashes birds.

How do I live?
I am fuzzy ear
& achling knee
redistricting.

Poor policy...
who could bare
ly mouth their
mother's name.

America's Art:
astonishing as
is astonishing
as astonishing

Welcome I love
you Welcome we
fully expected
their welcome.

America that's
America when's
America then's
their America.

How it shines:
Golden tulips.
When it shows:
Silver sticks.

Hap happy love
hap hap hap ha
ppy love happy
love love love

FriendsFriends
MendingMending
BendingBending
Vended, Vended

The playground
if playgrounds
my playgrounds
are boundless.

She felt a pea
whose mind was
set to viewing
all this land.

Golden Sunsets
Cinnamon Kitty
Neo-Electrical
Baseball City.

America has to
by ought frame
should launder
cause it could

How she grows:
Silver Spurs--
How it clicked
--Four Devils.

Handkerchiefs.
Returnstiling.
The Whistling.
ThePaperDrift.

Just about the
time that that
was said their
child laughed.

Eventually The
By Noting When
Blue eyes Blue
Black is Black

AbrahamLincoln
& Washingtons;
that Jefferson
was Jefferson.

Then she threw
open her heart
like a pigeon,
like an arrow.

Spanish Dancer
Spilling Esses
Filling Dishes
Soon Confesses

Silverer Moon.
I see America,
as if America,
sees me too...

My playgrounds
are boundless.
How she grows:
Handkerchiefs.

How do I live?
I like America
's paint dries
a partial view

www.ingramcontent.com/pod-product-compliance
Lightning Source LLC
Chambersburg PA
CBHW031335040426
42443CB00005B/350